Joplin for Students

7 Graded Arrangements for Intermediate Pianists

Arranged by

Carol Matz

Scott Joplin (1868–1917), a renowned African-American composer and pianist, is often referred to as the "King of Ragtime." He studied classical music as a boy, and had a remarkable ability to improvise at the piano. As a teenager, Joplin worked as a traveling musician before attending college in Sedalia, Missouri. During this time, he began composing and had his first pieces published, including "Maple Leaf Rag." Joplin went on to become the greatest and most influential of all ragtime composers, with 44 ragtime pieces, two operas, and a ragtime ballet.

Joplin for Students, Book 3, is written at the intermediate level. Along with some of Joplin's most popular rags, this collection also contains slower, more lyrical compositions, including an accessible arrangement of the beautiful serenade "Solace." The pieces appear in approximate order of difficulty. Joplin's original scores often used the tempo marking "Not fast;" therefore, students should avoid playing these pieces too fast (a common performance error with ragtime).

Alfred Music Publishing Co., Inc.
P.O. Box 10003
Van Nuys, CA 91410-0003
alfred.com

ISBN-10: 0-7390-7105-X
ISBN-13: 978-0-7390-7105-2

Cover portrait by Sarah Vaughan

MAPLE LEAF RAG

Scott Joplin
Arranged by Carol Matz

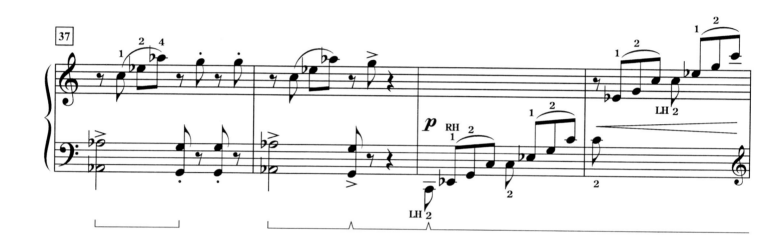

ROSE LEAF RAG

(A Ragtime Two Step)

Scott Joplin
Arranged by Carol Matz

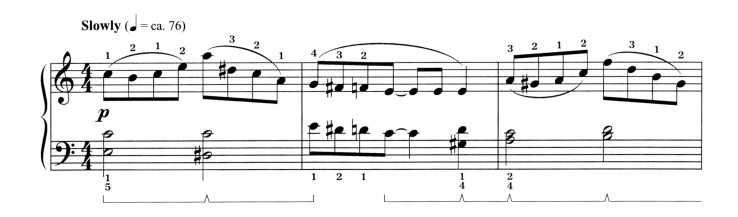

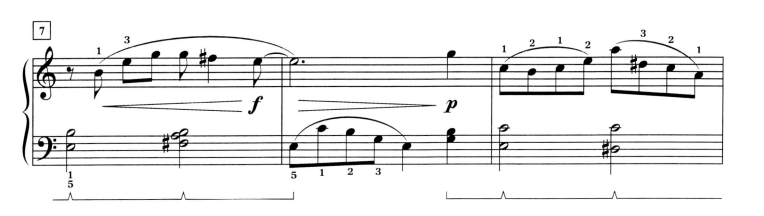

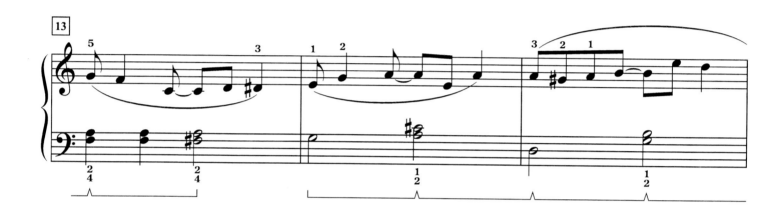

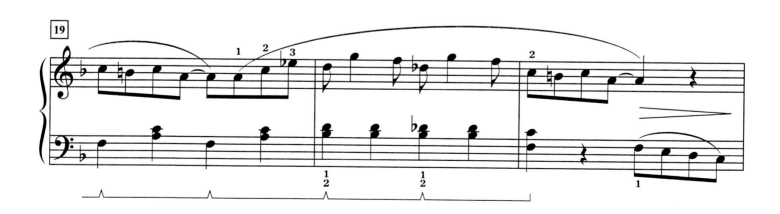

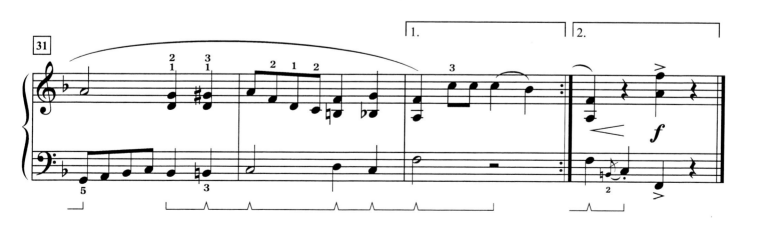

PINE APPLE RAG

Scott Joplin
Arranged by Carol Matz

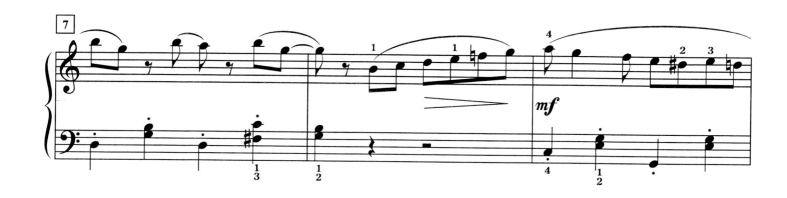

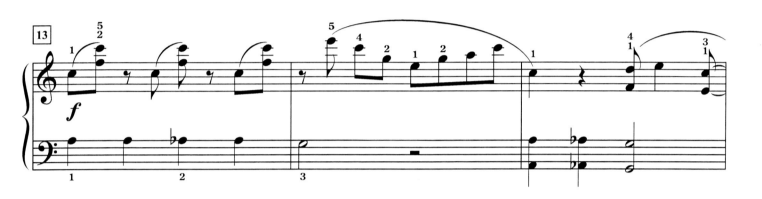

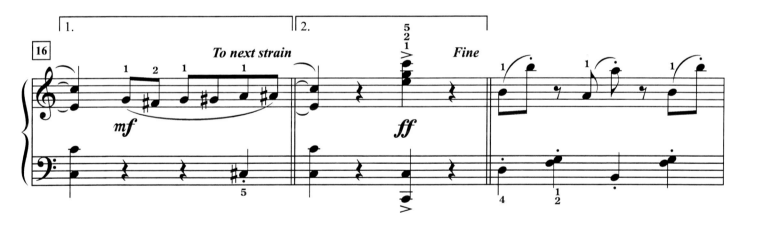

D.C. al Fine

ELITE SYNCOPATIONS

Scott Joplin
Arranged by Carol Matz

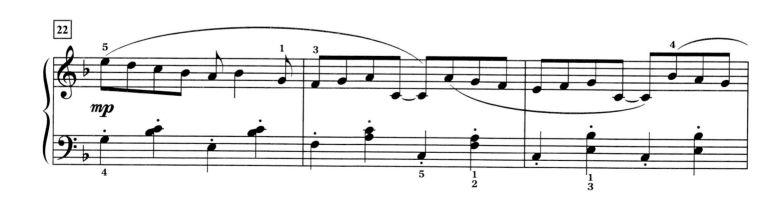

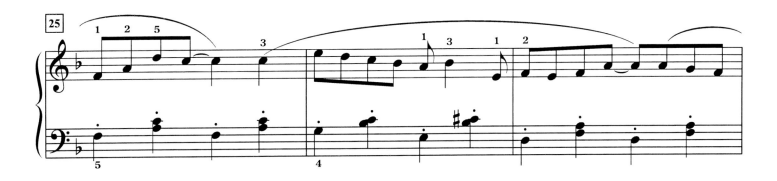

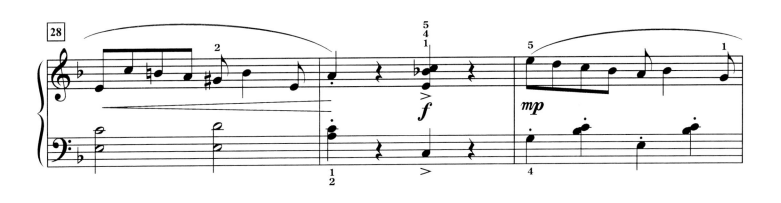

D.S. al Fine

THE ENTERTAINER

(A Ragtime Two Step)

Scott Joplin
Arranged by Carol Matz

* The pedal is optional.

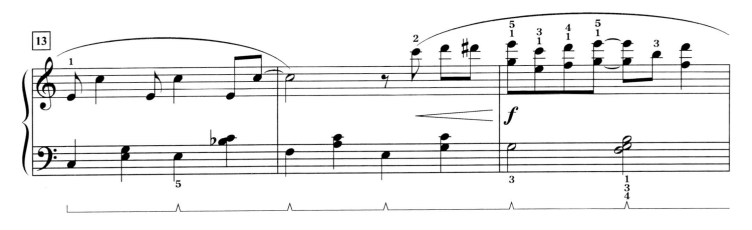

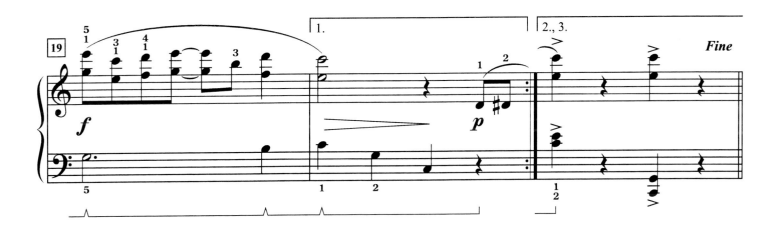

HELIOTROPE BOUQUET

(A Slow Drag Two Step)

Scott Joplin and Louis Chauvin
Arranged by Carol Matz

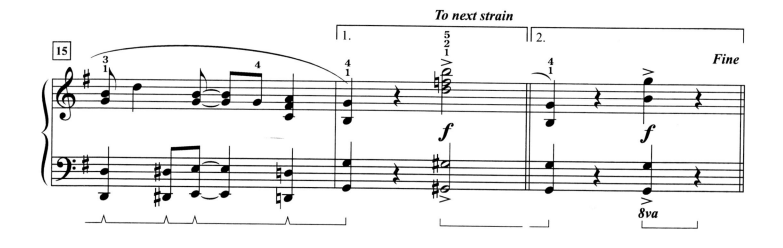

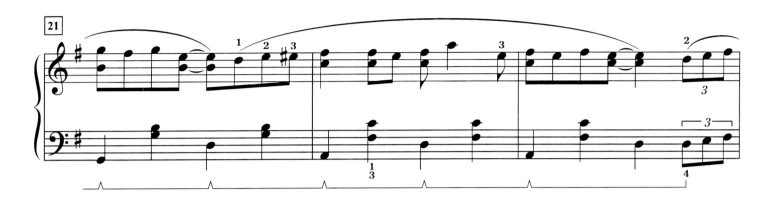

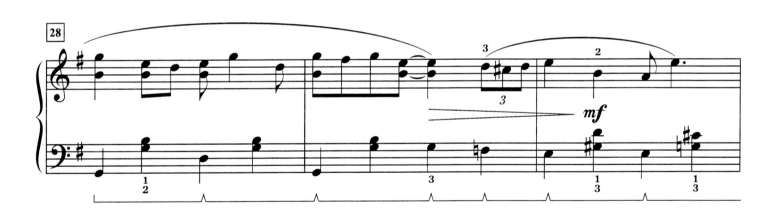

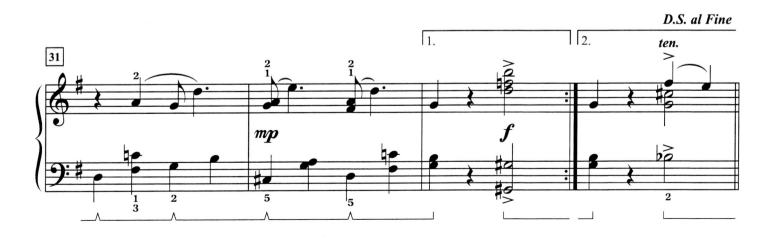

SOLACE

(A Mexican Serenade)

Scott Joplin
Arranged by Carol Matz

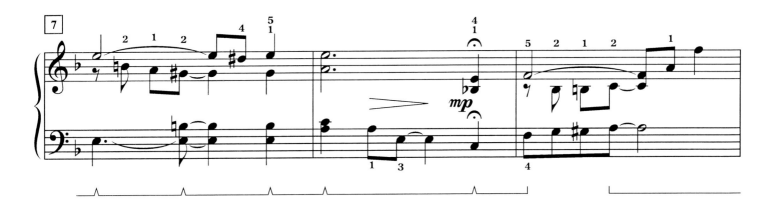

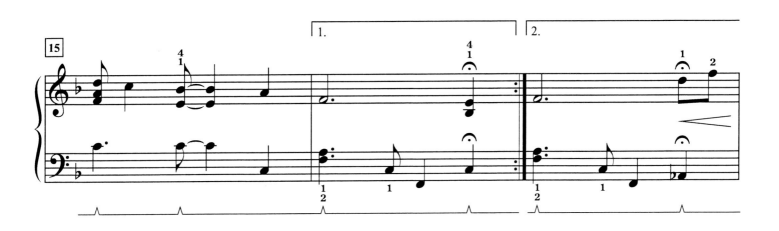

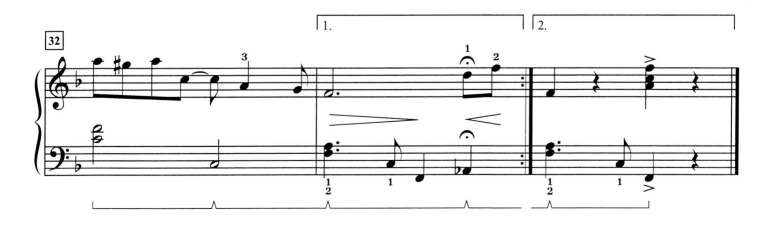